365 Days of Positive Thinking:

Volume 2

A motivational quote-a-day from the world's most inspiring women.

BELLANOVA

MELBOURNE · SOFIA · BERLIN

365 Days of Positive Thinking: Volume 2: A quote-a-day from Inspiring Women

Copyright © 2022 by Bellanova Books

www.bellanovabooks.com

All rights reserved. No part of this book may be reproduced in any form by any electronic or mechanical means including photocopying, recording, or information storage and retrieval without permission in writing from the author.

ISBN: 978-619-7695-04-5
Imprint: Bellanova Books

Introduction

Thank you for purchasing this book. In my life, positive quotes have had a huge influence on my motivation. It's incredible what a few words can do for you — it can take you from chronic procrastinator to achieving some of your greatest work. They are uplifting, inspiring and thought-provoking.

In the second volume of this book, I have hand-picked 365 of my favorite motivational quotes from **inspiring women**— that's one for each day of the year. How you use this book is entirely up to you, but I find that it's worth grabbing a pen or some Post-It notes and marking the quotes that really resonate with you. Everyone is affected differently by different words — and also at different times of our lives, and when you find one that motivates you personally, you want to be able to access it whenever you're feeling flat.

Perhaps you want to pick some of your favorites, write them down and place them beside your bed, in your purse or next to your desk. Whatever works for you! You can also use the page on the right to take note of some of your favorites.

My favorite quotes...

Day 1

"Don't live life in the past lane."

—Samantha Ettus

Day 2

"I am not free while any woman is unfree, even when her shackles are very different from my own."

—*Audre Lorde*

Day 3

"If you don't risk anything, you risk even more."

—Erica Jong

Day 4

"You could certainly say that I've never underestimated myself. There's nothing wrong with being ambitious."

—Angela Merkel

Day 5

"Doubt is a killer. You just have to know who you are and what you stand for."

—Jennifer Lopez

Day 6

"The price way pay for being ourselves is worth it."

—*Eartha Kitt*

Day 7

"Learn from the mistakes of others. You can't live long enough to make them all yourself."

—*Eleanor Roosevelt*

Day 8

"My coach said I run like a girl. And I said if he ran a little faster, he could too."

—Mia Hamm

Day 9

"You can't be that kid standing at the top of the waterslide, overthinking it. You have to go down the chute."

—*Tina Fey*

Day 10

"It's really important for us to be unapologetic. To be bold. To be brave. And to take huge risks."

—Awkwafina

Day 11

"Always aim high, work hard, and care deeply about what you believe in."

—Hillary Clinton

Day 12

"Limit your 'always' and your 'nevers'."

—Amy Poehler

Day 13

"All the people who knock me down only inspire me to do better."

—Selena Gomez

Day 14

"Hold onto your old friends. Kiss your mama. Admit what your dreams are."

—Maya Rudolph

Day 15

"The most effective way to do it, is to do it."

—Amelia Earhart

Day 16

"Always be a first-rate version of yourself instead of a second-rate version of somebody else."

—Judy Garland

Day 17

"Girls should never be afraid to be smart."

— *Emma Watson*

Day 18

"Those who have a strong sense of love and belonging have the courage to be imperfect."

—Brené Brown

Day 19

"We need women who are so strong they can be gentle, so educated they can be humble, so fierce they can be compassionate, so passionate they can be rational, and so disciplined they can be free."

—Kavita Ramdas

Day 20

"A flower does not think of competing with the flower next to it. It just blooms."

—Hannah Lavon

Day 21

"In order to be irreplaceable one must always be different."

—*Coco Chanel*

Day 22

"Step out of the history that is holding you back. Step into the new story you are willing to create."

—Oprah Winfrey

Day 23

"You have to trust in what you think. If you splinter yourself and try to please everyone, you can't."

—*Annie Leibovitz*

Day 24

"A strong woman stands up for herself. A stronger woman stands up for everybody else."

—Unknown

Day 25

"If you can dance and be free and not be embarrassed, you can rule the world."

—Amy Poehler

Day 26

"Just because you are blind, and unable to see my beauty doesn't mean it does not exist."

—Margaret Cho

Day 27

"There is no gate, no lock, no bolt that you can set upon the freedom of my mind."

—Virginia Woolf

Day 28

"You must love and care for yourself because that's when the best comes out."

—Tina Turner

Day 29

"What you do makes a difference, and you have to decide what kind of difference you want to make."

—Jane Goodall

Day 30

"I was smart enough to go through any door that opened."

—Joan Rivers

Day 31

"Beware of monotony; it's the mother of all the deadly sins."

—Edith Wharton

Day 32

"If you don't get out of the box you've been raised in, you won't understand how much bigger the world is."

—Angelina Jolie

Day 33

"I am no longer accepting the things I cannot change. I am changing the things I cannot accept."

—Angela Davis

Day 34

"Be messy and complicated and afraid and show up anyway."

—*Glennon Doyle Melton*

Day 35

"She does not know what the future holds, but she is grateful for slow and steady growth."

—Morgan Harper Nichols

Day 36

"I attribute my success to this: I never gave or took any excuse."

—Florence Nightingale

Day 37

"Girls are capable of doing everything men are capable of doing. Sometimes they have more imagination than men."

—Katherine Johnson

Day 38

"Nothing is worth more than laughter. It is strength to laugh and to abandon oneself, to be light."

—Frida Kahlo

Day 39

"I am learning every day to allow the space between where I am and where I want to be to inspire me and not terrify me."

—Tracee Ellis Ross

Day 40

"You have to have confidence in your ability, and then be tough enough to follow through."

—Rosalynn Carter

Day 41

"You must know that you can do this. You are strong. And you will make it. Just hang on and keep believing in yourself, always."

—*Heather A. Stillufsen*

Day 42

"I'd never been a good damsel in distress. I was a 'hands-on' damsel."

—Jennifer Armintrout

Day 43

"If you don't see a clear path for what you want, sometimes you have to make it yourself."

—Mindy Kaling

Day 44

"Good girls go to heaven, bad girls go everywhere."

—Mae West

Day 45

"The most common way people give up their power is by thinking they don't have any."

—*Alice Walker*

Day 46

"We must reject not only the stereotypes that others hold of us, but also the stereotypes that we hold of ourselves."

—*Shirley Chisholm*

Day 47

"Think like a queen. A queen if not afraid to fail. Failure is another stepping stone to greatness."

-Oprah Winfrey

Day 48

"Don't compromise yourself. You are all you've got. There is no yesterday, no tomorrow, it's all the same day."

—Janis Joplin

Day 49

"Do not stop thinking of life as an adventure. You have no security unless you can live bravely, excitingly, imaginatively; unless you can choose a challenge instead of competence."

-Eleanor Roosevelt

Day 50

"Real change, enduring change, happens one step at a time."

-Ruth Bader Ginsburg

Day 51

"For every failure, there's an alternative course of action. You just have to find it. When you come to a roadblock, take a detour."

—Mary Kay Ash

Day 52

"I always wanted to be a femme fatale. Even when I was a young girl, I never really wanted to be a girl. I wanted to be a woman."

—*Diane Von Furstenberg*

Day 53

"Surround yourself with people and things that inspire you. Learn everything you can."

—Jameela Jamil

Day 54

"Don't be afraid. Be focused. Be determined. Be hopeful. Be empowered."

—*Michelle Obama*

Day 55

"I'd rather regret the risks that didn't work out than the chances I didn't take at all."

—Simone Biles

Day 56

"They'll tell you you're too loud, that you need to wait your turn and ask the right people for permission. Do it anyway."

–Alexandria Ocasio Cortez

Day 57

Do not tame the wolf inside you just because you've met someone who doesn't have the courage to handle you.

—Belle Estreller

Day 58

"Strong women don't play the victim. Don't make themselves look pitiful and don't point fingers. They stand and they deal."

-Mandy Hale

Day 59

"I figure, if a girl wants to be a legend, she should go ahead and be one."

—Calamity Jane

Day 60

I am the heat of a wildfire, the race of a storm. I am strong. Delicate things are pretty cute, even. I am not delicate. I am wild, fierce and unpredictable. I am breathtaking. I am beautiful. I am sacred.

—*Brooke Hampton*

Day 61

"Above all, be the heroine of your life, not the victim."

—*Nora Ephron, writer*

Day 62

"Find your 'why' so that you have the strength and resilience to push through those times when everything else is telling you no."

—Lisa Wimberger

Day 63

"Every time someone writes that I play 'strong women' what they're implying is that most women aren't. How about I just play well-written parts?"

—Jessica Chastain

Day 64

"You have to believe in yourself when no one else does."

—*Serena Williams*

Day 65

"In a world that wants women to whisper, I choose to yell."

—*Luvvie Ajayi*

Day 66

"Ditch the dream and be a doer."

—*Shonda Rhimes*

Day 67

"My experiences remind me that it's those black clouds that make the blue skies even more beautiful."

—Kelly Clarkson

Day 68

"Striving for excellence motivates you; striving for perfection is demoralizing."

—Dr. Harriet Braiker

Day 69

"I'm always perpetually out of my comfort zone."

—Tory Burch

Day 70

"No woman should be told she can't make decisions about her own body. When women's rights are under attack, we fight back."

—Kamala Harris

Day 71

"You only live once, but if you do it right, once is enough."

—Mae West

Day 72

"You need to know that you're enough – a mantra that has now ingrained itself so deeply within me that not a day goes by without hearing it chime in my head."

—*Meghan Markle*

Day 73

"I believe in being strong when everything seems to be going wrong, I believe that happy girls are the prettiest girls. I believe that tomorrow is another day, and I believe in miracles."

-Audrey Hepburn

Day 74

"I would rather be thought of as smart, capable, strong and passionate than beautiful. These things all persist long after beauty fades."

—Cassandra Duffy

Day 75

"Own yourself, woman."

—Toni Morrison

Day 76

"Be strong enough to stand alone, smart enough to know when you need help, and brave enough to ask for it."

—Ziad K. Abdelnour

Day 77

"One cannot accomplish anything without fanaticism."

—Eva Perón

Day 78

"If you don't like the road you're walking, start paving another one."

—Dolly Parton

Day 79

"No matter how difficult and painful it may be, nothing sounds as good to the soul as the truth."

—Martha Beck

Day 80

"A lot of people are afraid to say what they want. That's why they don't get what they want."

—*Madonna*

Day 81

"There is a stubbornness about me that can never bear to be frightened at the will of others. My courage always rises at every attempt to intimidate me."

—Jane Austen

Day 82

"We do not need magic to transform our world. We carry all of the power we need inside ourselves already."

—J.K. Rowling

Day 83

"Like art, revolutions come from combining what exists into what has never existed before."

—*Gloria Steinem*

Day 84

"[Unlikeable women] accept the consequences of their choices, and those consequences become stories worth reading."

—*Roxane Gay*

Day 85

"A strong woman understands that the gifts such as logic, decisiveness, and strength are just as feminine as intuition and emotional connection. She values and uses all of her gifts."

—Nancy Rathburn

Day 86

"I think the best role models for women are people who are fruitfully and confidently themselves, who bring light into the world."

—Meryl Streep

Day 87

"If you find someone you love in your life, then hang on to that love."

—Princess Diana

Day 88

"There's something so special about a woman who dominates in a man's world. It takes a certain grace, strength, intelligence, fearlessness, and the nerve to never take no for an answer."

—Rihanna

Day 89

"Figure out who you are separate from your family, and the man or woman you're in a relationship with. Find who you are in this world and what you need to feel good alone. I think that's the most important thing in life. Find a sense of self because with that, you can do anything else."

—*Angelina Jolie*

Day 90

"A huge part of being a feminist is giving other women the freedom to make choices you might not necessarily make yourself."

—Lena Dunham

Day 91

"I can't think of any better representation of beauty than someone who is unafraid to be herself."

—Emma Stone

Day 92

"Just don't give up trying to do what you really want to do. Where there is love and inspiration, I don't think you can go wrong."

—*Ella Fitzgerald*

Day 93

"Security is mostly a superstition. Life is either a daring adventure or nothing."

—*Helen Keller*

Day 94

"You are more powerful than you know; you are beautiful just as you are."

—*Melissa Etheridge*

Day 95

"If I stop to kick every barking dog I am not going to get where I'm going."

—Jackie Joyner-Kersee

Day 96

"You are the one that possesses the keys to your being. You carry the passport to your own happiness."

—*Diane von Furstenberg*

Day 97

"I always thought that people told you that you're beautiful–that this was a title that was bestowed upon you ... I think that it's time to take this power into our own hands and to say, 'You know what? I'm beautiful. I just am. And that's my light. I'm just a beautiful woman.'

—Margaret Cho

Day 98

"Make the most of yourself by fanning the tiny, inner sparks of possibility into flames of achievement."

—Golda Meir

Day 99

"Don't look at your feet to see if you are doing it right. Just dance."

—Anne Lamott

Day 100

"In the future, there will be no female leaders. There will just be leaders."

—*Sheryl Sandberg*

Day 101

"This is your moment. Own it."

—Oprah Winfrey

Day 102

"A feminist is anyone who recognizes the equality and full humanity of women and men."

—Gloria Steinem

Day 103

"Each time a woman stands up for herself, without knowing it possibly, without claiming it, she stands up for all women."

—*Maya Angelou*

Day 104

"My natural thing is to be a problem solver. And so when things happen to me, I'm, like, 'Walk away.' Because that's how I was my entire life. I've been in the storm too long for that to shake me."

—Mariah Carey

Day 105

"Do we want to progress? If we want to progress, let women be all they can be. Don't get in their way."

—Danai Gurira

Day 106

"You will not determine my story. I will."

—*Amy Schumer*

Day 107

"Your unique magnificence is blinding in its beauty."

—Kim E. Woods

Day 108

"Don't be like the rest of them darling."

—*Coco Chanel*

Day 109

"We forget we have the right to have a voice. You have the right to get what you ask for. And if you say nothing, you're going to have zero percent chance to fix it."

—Joy Mangano

Day 110

"No one is going to tell you all the things you want to hear all the time. You have to know them yourself."

—*Busy Philipps*

Day 111

"Men selectively listen. When that happened, I'd stop the conversation and say, 'Do you realize I said that 10 minutes ago?' Women have to take responsibility for the dynamic around them. You can't just say, 'Woe is me.'"

—Maggie Wilderotter

Day 112

"Boss up and change your life."

—Lizzo

Day 113

"You can always find a solution if you try hard enough."

—Lori Greiner

Day 114

"Stay committed and consistent and you will achieve your goals. Never give up."

—Kelly Rowland

Day 115

"If people are doubting how far you can go, go so far that you can't hear them anymore."

—*Michele Ruiz*

Day 116

"Instead of looking at the past, I put myself ahead twenty years and try to look at what I need to do now in order to get there then."

—*Diana Ross*

Day 117

"I believe the rights of women and girls is the unfinished business of the 21st century."

—Hillary Clinton

Day 118

"We need to reshape our own perception of how we view ourselves. We have to step up as women and take the lead."

—Beyoncé

Day 119

"You deserve to be here. You deserve to exist. You deserve to take up space in this world of men."

—MacKenzi Lee

Day 120

"I'd rather regret the things I've done than regret the things I haven't done."

—*Lucille Ball*

Day 121

"No one changes the world who isn't obsessed."

—Billie Jean King

Day 122

"On my own, I will just create, and if it works, it works, and if it doesn't, I'll create something else. I don't have any limitations on what I think I could do or be."

—*Oprah Winfrey*

Day 123

"Your mindset can control you, or you can control it. It can reward you, or it can own you. You get to decide. What are you choosing?"

—Leila Kashani

Day 124

"Why not take a chance and bet on happiness?

—*Jenny Han*

Day 125

"A strong woman looks a challenge dead in the eye and gives it a wink."

—Gina Carey

Day 126

"The warrior knows that her heartbreak is her map."

—Glennon Doyle Melton

Day 127

"We have to let go of the idea of balance in order to move toward the life we want. To do that, we need to recognize the stories we are telling ourselves that are holding us back. And sometimes ... we just have to stop telling ourselves our old stories."

—Tonya Dalton

Day 128

"Without an open-minded mind, you can never be a great success."

—Martha Stewart

Day 129

"You never know if you can actually do something against all odds until you actually do it."

—Abby Wambach

Day 130

"Careers are a jungle gym, not a ladder."

—Sheryl Sandberg

Day 131

"It doesn't matter when you start, it doesn't matter what anyone else is doing. All that matters is that you truly follow your own path, your own way, at your own pace. Be kind to yourself and others, and follow your intuition always. That is real bravery."

—*Diana Schneider*

Day 132

"Everything is figureoutable."

—Marie Forleo

Day 133

"Once you know who you are, you don't have to worry anymore."

—*Nikki Giovanni*

Day 134

"There were times I was underestimated a lot. It gave me a unique benefit."

—Elaine Welteroth

Day 135

"Responsibility to yourself means refusing to let others do your thinking, talking, and naming for you; it means learning to respect and use your own brains and instincts; hence, grappling with hard work."

—Adrienne Rich

Day 136

"You can waste your lives drawing lines. Or you can live your life crossing them."

—Shonda Rhimes

Day 137

"Imperfections are beauty, madness is genius, and it's better to be absolutely ridiculous than absolutely boring."

—Marilyn Monroe

Day 138

"Optimism is the faith that leads to achievement."

—Helen Keller

Day 139

"I have stood on a mountain of no's for one yes."

—B. Smith

Day 140

"Done is better than perfect."

—Sheryl Sandberg

Day 141

"I firmly believe you never should spend your time being the former anything."

—Condoleezza Rice

Day 142

"Change your life today. Don't gamble on the future, act now, without delay."

—Simone de Beauvoir

Day 143

"Owning our story can be hard but not nearly as difficult as spending our lives running from it."

—Brené Brown

Day 144

"If your home environment is good and peaceful and easy, your life is better and easier."

—Lori Greiner

Day 145

"The best thing to hold onto in life is each other."

—Audrey Hepburn

Day 146

"If you can't go straight ahead, you go around the corner."

—Cher

Day 147

"It's one of the greatest gifts you can give yourself, to forgive. Forgive everybody."

—*Maya Angelou*

Day 148

"I choose to make the rest of my life the best of my life."

—*Louise Hay*

Day 149

"Spread love everywhere you go. Let no one ever come to you without leaving happier."

—*Mother Teresa*

Day 150

"Find ecstasy in life; the mere sense of living is joy enough."

—*Emily Dickinson*

Day 151

"When we speak we are afraid our words will not be heard or welcomed. But when we are silent, we are still afraid. So it is better to speak."

—*Audre Lorde*

Day 152

"Take criticism seriously, but not personally. If there is truth or merit in the criticism, try to learn from it. Otherwise, let it roll right off you."

—Hillary Clinton

Day 153

"When I'm hungry, I eat. When I'm thirsty, I drink. When I feel like saying something, I say it."

—Madonna

Day 154

"Never apologize for being a powerful woman."

—Unknown

Day 155

"It's not the absence of fear, it's overcoming it. Sometimes you've got to blast through and have faith."

—Emma Watson

Day 156

"There are two kinds of people, those who do the work and those who take the credit. Try to be in the first group; there is less competition there."

—Indira Gandhi

Day 157

"She was a wild one; always stomping on eggshells that everyone else tip-toed on."

—Kaitlin Foster

Day 158

"The woman who doesn't require validation from anyone is the most feared individual on the planet."

—*Mohadesa Najumi*

Day 159

"I am proud of the woman I am today, because I went through one hell of a time becoming her."

—*Unknown*

Day 160

"Women have discovered that they cannot rely on men's chivalry to give them justice."

—Helen Keller

Day 161

"I love to see a young girl go out and grab the world by the lapels. Life's a bitch. You've got to go out and kick ass."

—*Maya Angelou*

Day 162

"I am a woman and a warrior. If you think I can't be both, you've been lied to."

—Jennifer Zeynab Joukhadar

Day 163

"I want to build a community where women of all races can communicate and … continue to support and take care of each other. I want to give women a space to feel their own strength and tell their stories. That is power."

—*Beyoncé*

Day 164

"Learn to embrace your own unique Prettiness, celebrate your unique gifts with confidence. Your imperfections are actually a gift."

—Kerry Washington

Day 165

"Strong women don't have 'attitudes', we have standards."

—Marilyn Monroe

Day 166

"Dying seems less sad than having lived too little."

—Gloria Steinem

Day 167

"Avoiding danger is no safer in the long run than outright exposure. The fearful are caught as often as the bold."

—Helen Keller

Day 168

"Women are leaders everywhere you look—from the CEO who runs a Fortune 500 company to the housewife who raises her children and heads her household. Our country was built by strong women, and we will continue to break down walls and defy stereotypes."

—Nancy Pelosi

Day 169

"I don't care what you think about me. I don't think about you at all."

—Coco Chanel

Day 170

"If you're one of those people who has that little voice in the back of her mind saying, 'Maybe I could do [fill in the blank],' don't tell it to be quiet. Give it a little room to grow, and try to find an environment it can grow in."

—Reese Witherspoon

Day 171

"Once I learned to like me more than others did, then I didn't have to worry about being the funniest or the most popular or the prettiest. I was the best me and I only ever tried to be that."

—*Issa Rae*

Day 172

"A strong woman knows she has strength enough for the journey, but a woman of strength knows it is in the journey where she will become strong."

—*Unknown*

Day 173

"I do not try to dance better than anyone else. I only try to dance better than myself."

—*Arianna Huffington*

Day 174

"Inner peace is possible when you practice outward gratitude."

—Emily Lynn Paulson

Day 175

"Hope is the most exciting thing there is in life."

—Mandy Moore

Day 176

"We need women at all levels, including the top, to change the dynamic, reshape the conversation, to make sure women's voices are heard and heeded, not overlooked and ignored."

—*Sheryl Sandberg*

Day 177

"She remembered who she was and the game changed."

—Lalah Deliah

Day 178

"Nothing is impossible, the word itself says 'I'm possible!'"

—Audrey Hepburn

Day 179

"Women have to harness their power—it's absolutely true. It's just learning not to take the first no. And if you can't go straight ahead, you go around the corner."

—Cher

Day 180

"When someone tells you that you can't, figure out how you can."

—*Clarice Lam*

Day 181

"My husband always tells me that I'm the most unrelenting person he's ever met, and it's true. If I make a commitment to something, I will stick to it no matter what."

—Jenny Craig

Day 182

"Success is getting what you want. Happiness is wanting what you get."

—Ingrid Bergman

Day 183

"Choose your dream. Work to the extreme."

—Tyra Banks

Day 184

"Without leaps of imagination, or dreaming, we lose the excitement of possibilities. Dreaming, after all, is a form of planning."

—*Gloria Steinem*

Day 185

"Life is not so much what you accomplish as what you overcome."

—Robin Roberts

Day 186

"Value your time so you can spend time doing what you value."

—*Melissa St. Clair*

Day 187

"Invite people into your life that don't look or think like you."

—Mellody Hobson

Day 188

"Success requires competence and confidence. You must be good at what you do; and you must speak up and take credit for your work. One or the other just won't cut it."

—*Michelle Bomberger*

Day 189

"Run your own race. Don't be distracted by what others are doing. Set and go after your own goals."

—*Jen Gouldstone*

Day 190

"Women must try to do things as men have tried. When they fail, their failure must be but a challenge to others."

—Amelia Earhart

Day 191

"One of the biggest qualities is having an awareness outside of yourself, and understanding that the world doesn't revolve around your needs."

—*Brie Larson*

Day 192

"I can't think of any better representation of beauty than someone who is unafraid to be yourself."

—*Emma Stone*

Day 193

"If you're always trying to be normal, you will never know how amazing you can be."

—*Maya Angelou*

Day 194

"There's power in allowing yourself to be known and heard, in owning your unique story, in using your authentic voice."

—*Michelle Obama*

Day 195

"You cannot shake hands with a clenched fist."

—*Indira Gandhi*

Day 196

"Have no fear of perfection; you'll never reach it."

—Marie Curie

Day 197

"Always aim high, work hard, and care deeply about what you believe in. And, when you stumble, keep faith. And, when you're knocked down, get right back up and never listen to anyone who says you can't or shouldn't go on."

—*Hillary Clinton*

Day 198

"I've had to learn to fight all my life – got to learn to keep smiling. If you smile things will work out."

—Serena Williams

Day 199

"You don't make progress by standing on the sidelines whimpering and complaining. You make progress by implementing ideas."

—*Shirley Chisholm*

Day 200

"I was a person with dignity and self-respect, and I should not set my sights lower than anybody else just because I was black."

—*Rosa Parks*

Day 201

"Technique and ability alone do not get you to the top; it is the willpower that is most important."

—*Junko Tabei*

Day 202

"Some people are old at 18 and some are young at 90. Time is a concept that humans created."

—Yoko Ono

Day 203

"Let us make our future now, and let us make our dreams tomorrow's reality."

—*Malala Yousafzai*

Day 204

"You don't have to play masculine to be a strong woman."

—Mary Elizabeth Winstead

Day 205

"If your actions create a legacy that inspires others to dream more, learn more, do more and become more, then, you are an excellent leader."

—Dolly Parton

Day 206

"Don't let anyone rob you of your imagination, your creativity, or your curiosity. It's your place in the world; it's your life. Go on and do all you can with it, and make it the life you want to live."

—*Mae C. Jemison*

Day 207

"The Prettiness of being a feminist is that you get to be whatever you want. And that's the point."

—*Shonda Rhimes*

Day 208

"There will be people who say to you, 'You are out of your lane'. They are burdened by only having the capacity to see what has always been instead of what can be. But don't let that burden you."

—*Kamala Harris*

Day 209

"Everyone has inside of her a piece of good news. The good news is that you don't know how great you can be, how much you can love, what you can accomplish, and what your potential is."

—*Anne Frank*

Day 210

As for my girls, I'll raise them to think they breathe fire.

—Jessica Kirkland

Day 211

"Life is tough, my darling. But so are you."

—Stephanie Bennet Henry

Day 212

"My mission in life is not merely to survive but to thrive and to do so with some passion, some compassion, some humor, and some style."

—*Maya Angelou*

Day 213

"I found that ultimately if you truly pour your heart into what you believe in—even if it makes you vulnerable—amazing things can and will happen."

—*Emma Watson*

Day 214

Women are always saying, 'We can do anything that men can do.' But men should be saying, 'We can do anything that women can do.'

—*Gloria Steinem*

Day 215

"A girl should be two things: who and what she wants."

—Coco Chanel

Day 216

"A revolutionary woman can't have no reactionary man."

—Assata Shakur

Day 217

"When the whole world is silent, even one voice becomes powerful."

—Malala Yousafzai

"When you get into a tight place and everything goes against you, till it seems as though you could not hold on a minute longer, never give up then, for that is just the place and time that the tide will turn."

—Harriet Beecher Stowe

Day 219

"One of the secrets to staying young is to always do things you don't know how to do, to keep learning."

—Ruth Reichl

Day 220

"Women don't need to find a voice, they have a voice, and they need to feel empowered to use it, and people need to be encouraged to listen."

—*Meghan Markle*

Day 221

"I'm a feminist. I've been a female for a long time now. It'd be stupid not to be on my own side."

-Maya Angelou

Day 221

"I am too intelligent, too demanding, and too resourceful for anyone to be able to take charge of me entirely. No one knows me or loves me completely. I have only myself"

—Simone de Beauvoir

Day 223

"All careers go up and down like friendships, like marriages, like anything else, and you can't bat a thousand all the time."

—Julie Andrews

Day 224

"Courage, sacrifice, determination, commitment, toughness, heart, talent, guts. That's what little girls are made of; the heck with sugar and spice."

—*Bethany Hamilton*

Day 225

"I'm not going to limit myself just because people won't accept the fact that I can do something else."

—Dolly Parton

Day 226

"Be first and be lonely."

—Ginni Rometty

Day 227

"Drama is very important in life: You have to come on with a bang. You never want to go out with a whimper."

—*Julia Childs*

Day 228

"One of the most courageous things you can do is identify yourself, know who you are, what you believe in and where you want to go."

—*Sheila Murray Bethel*

Day 229

"A really strong woman accepts the war she went through and is ennobled by her scars."

—Carly Simon

Day 230

"I can promise you that women working together – linked, informed and educated – can bring peace and prosperity to this forsaken planet."

—Isabelle Allende

Day 231

"Stay strong. Stand up. Have a voice."

—Shawn Johnson

Day 232

"I am thankful for my struggle because, without it, I wouldn't have stumbled across my strength."

—Alex Elle

Day 233

"A woman is the full circle. Within her is the power to create, nurture and transform."

—Diane Mariechild

Day 234

"I learned compassion from being discriminated against. Everything bad that's ever happened to me has taught me compassion."

—Ellen DeGeneres

Day 235

"You can be the lead in your own life."

—Kerry Washington

Day 236

"A good compromise is one where everybody makes a contribution."

—Angela Merkel

Day 237

"A surplus of effort could overcome a deficit of confidence."

—*Sonia Sotomayor*

Day 238

"If you just set out to be liked, you would be prepared to compromise on anything at any time, and you would achieve nothing."

—Margaret Thatcher

Day 239

"The world needs strong women. Women who will lift and build others, who will love and be loved, women who live bravely, both tender and fierce, women of indomitable will."

—Amy Tenney

Day 240

"I've come to believe that each of us has a personal calling that's as unique as a fingerprint – and that the best way to succeed is to discover what you love and then find a way to offer it to others in the form of service, working hard, and also allowing the energy of the universe to lead you."

—Oprah Winfrey

Day 241

"The next decade cannot be a decade of confrontation and contention. It cannot be East vs. West. It cannot be men vs. women. It cannot be Islam vs. Christianity. That is what the enemies of dialogue want."

—Benazir Bhutto

Day 242

"Females are the most beautiful, gorgeous creatures in the whole world. And I think that we are gorgeous no matter what size we are."

—Alicia Keys

Day 243

"I say if I'm beautiful. I say if I'm strong."

—Amy Schumer

Day 244

"Courage doesn't always roar. Sometimes courage is the little voice at the end of the day that says I'll try again tomorrow."

—*Mary Anne Radmacher*

Day 245

"Once you figure out what respect tastes like, it tastes better than attention."

—P!nk

Day 246

"We have to teach our girls that they can reach as high as humanly possible."

—Beyoncé

Day 247

"If you're scared to speak up, it's usually a sign that you should."

—Tati Westbrook

Day 248

"I've had to learn to fight all my life – got to learn to keep smiling. If you smile things will work out."

—Serena Williams

Day 249

"More than ever, I am aware of the need to support and celebrate each other. I like to believe I am part of a global support group network of 3.4 billion. Imagine: if you can fall back on the 3.5 billion sisters, and the many good men who are with us, what could we possibly not achieve?"

—*Nicole Kidman*

Day 250

"I am always busy, which is perhaps the chief reason why I am always well."

—*Elizabeth Cady Stanton*

Day 251

"A girl should not expect special privileges because of her sex but neither should she adjust to prejudice and discrimination."

—Betty Friedan

Day 252

"I raise up my voice—not so I can shout but so that those without a voice can be heard... We cannot succeed when half of us are held back."

—*Malala Yousafzai*

Day 253

"What I wanted was to be allowed to do the thing in the world that I did best—which I believed then and believe now is the greatest privilege there is. When I did that, success found me."

—*Debbi Fields*

Day 254

"At the end of the day, we can endure much more than we think we can."

—Frida Kahlo

Day 255

"Don't ever make decisions based on fear. Make decisions based on hope and possibility. Make decisions based on what should happen, not what shouldn't."

—Michelle Obama

Day 256

"I don't have a feeling of inferiority. Never had. I'm as good as anybody, but no better."

—Katherine Johnson

Day 257

"My mother told me to be a lady. And for her, that meant be your own person, be independent."

—Ruth Bader Ginsberg

Day 258

"Fearlessness is like a muscle. I know from my own life that the more I exercise it the more natural it becomes to not let my fears run me."

—*Arianna Huffington*

Day 259

"You can be gorgeous at thirty, charming at forty, and irresistible for the rest of your life."

—*Coco Chanel*

Day 260

"Bring your whole self to the experience. Because the more we do that, the more that people get to see that, the more comfortable everybody's gonna be with it."

—*Bozoma Saint John*

Day 261

"Behind every great woman... is another great woman."

—Kate Hodges, Author

Day 262

"Do you want to meet the love of your life? Look in the mirror."

—Bryon Katie

Day 263

"Everyone shines, given the right lighting."

—Susan Cain

Day 264

"The challenge is not to be perfect…it's to be whole."

—Jane Fonda

Day 265

"I have learned over the years that when one's mind is made up, this diminishes fear; knowing what must be done does away with fear."

—Rosa Parks

Day 266

"You take your life in your own hands, and what happens? A terrible thing: no one to blame."

—Erica Jong

Day 267

"A woman without a man is like a fish without a bicycle."

—Irina Dunn

Day 268

"I really think a champion is defined not by their wins but by how they can recover when they fall."

—*Serena Williams*

Day 269

"Women should do for themselves what men have already done—occasionally what men have not done—thereby establishing themselves as persons, and perhaps encouraging other women toward greater independence of thought and action."

—*Amelia Earhart*

Day 270

"Tremendous amounts of talent are being lost to our society just because that talent wears a skirt."

—*Shirley Chisholm*

Day 271

"No one can make you feel inferior without your consent."

—Eleanor Roosevelt

Day 272

"Life is not easy for any of us. But what of that? We must have perseverance and above all confidence in ourselves. We must believe that we are gifted for something and that this thing must be attained."

—*Marie Curie*

Day 273

"Passion is the log that keeps the fire of purpose blazing."

—Oprah Winfrey

Day 274

"The most difficult thing is the decision to act. The rest is merely tenacity."

—Amelia Earhart

Day 275

"I never dreamed about success. I worked for it."

—*Estée Lauder*

Day 276

"Success is only meaningful and enjoyable if it feels like your own."

—*Michelle Obama*

Day 277

"I've been absolutely terrified every moment of my life—and I've never let it keep me from doing a single thing I wanted to do."

—*Georgia O'Keeffe*

Day 278

"Every moment wasted looking back, keeps us from moving forward...In this world and the world of tomorrow, we must go forward together or not at all."

—Hillary Clinton

Day 279

"Fight for the things that you care about, but do it in a way that will lead others to join you."

—Ruth Bader Ginsburg

Day 280

"Aging is not "lost youth" but a new stage of opportunity and strength."

—*Betty Friedan*

Day 281

"If you don't like something, change it. If you can't change it, change your attitude."

—Maya Angelou

"We are here, not because we are law-breakers; we are here in our efforts to become law-makers."

—Emmeline Pankhurst

Day 283

"Pursuing peace means rising above one's own wants, needs, and emotions."

—Benazir Bhutto

Day 284

"Social change is brought about by those who dare and act, who can think unconventionally and who can court unpopularity."

—*Indira Gandhi*

Day 285

"When you embrace your difference, your DNA, your look or heritage or religion or your unusual name, that's when you start to shine."

—*Bethenny Frankel*

Day 286

"I need to listen well so that I hear what is not said."

—Thuli Madonsela

Day 287

"When you're through changing, you're through."

—*Martha Stewart*

Day 288

"Normal is not something to aspire to, it's something to get away from."

—*Jodie Foster*

Day 289

"Cautious, careful people, always casting about to preserve their reputations can never effect a reform."

—Susan B. Anthony

Day 290

"You can't please everyone, and you can't make everyone like you."

—Katie Couric

Day 291

"I am an example of what is possible when girls from the very beginning of their lives are loved and nurtured by people around them. I was surrounded by extraordinary women in my life who taught me about quiet strength and dignity."

—Michelle Obama

Day 292

"I hate to hear you talk about all women as if they were fine ladies instead of rational creatures. None of us want to be in calm waters all our lives."

—Jane Austen

Day 293

"When I'm tired, I rest. I say, 'I can't be a superwoman today.'"

—*Jada Pinkett Smith*

Day 294

"Hard work keeps the wrinkles out of the mind and spirit."

—Helena Rubinstein

Day 295

"We're all water from different rivers, that's why it's so easy to meet; we're all water in this vast, vast ocean, someday we'll evaporate together."

—Yoko Ono

Day 296

"Do what you feel in your heart to be right—for you'll be criticized anyway."

—*Eleanor Roosevelt*

Day 297

"Successful people understand that you don't need to make things complicated."

—*Anne McKevitt*

Day 298

"Great minds discuss ideas; average minds discuss events; small minds discuss people."

—Eleanor Roosevelt

Day 299

"Change happens by listening and then starting a dialogue with the people who are doing something you don't believe is right."

—Jane Goodall

Day 300

"I've learned that making a 'living' is not the same as 'making a life.'"

—Maya Angelou

Day 301

We need to understand that there is no formula for how women should lead their lives. That is why we must respect the choices that each woman makes for herself and her family. Every woman deserves the chance to realize her God-given potential."

—*Hillary Clinton*

"You have to be careful when you're getting feedback because people will give you conflicting feedback all the time, but ultimately you end up following your own inner guide."

—Natalie Portman

Day 303

"We cannot solve a crisis without treating it as a crisis. [...] And if solutions within the system are so impossible to find, then maybe we should change the system itself?"

—Greta Thunberg

Day 304

"A woman with a voice is, by definition, a strong woman. But the search to find that voice can be remarkably difficult."

—*Melinda Gates*

Day 305

"It's not your job to be likeable. It's your job to be yourself. Someone will like you anyway."

—Chimamanda Ngozi Adichie

Day 306

"We need to get women to the point where they aren't apologizing. It is time to take ownership in our success."

—*Tory Burch*

Day 307

"If you're someone people count on, particularly in difficult moments, that's a sign of a life lived honorably."

—*Rachel Maddow*

Day 308

"Courage is like a muscle. We strengthen it by use."

—Ruth Gordon

Day 309

"The greatest danger to our future is apathy."

—*Jane Goodall*

Day 310

"To all the little girls who are watching this, never doubt that you are valuable and powerful, and deserving of every chance and opportunity in the world to pursue and achieve your own dreams."

—Hillary Clinton

Day 311

"The difference between successful people and others is how long they spend time feeling sorry for themselves."

—Barbara Corcoran

Day 312

"Ignore the glass ceiling and do your work. If you're focusing on the glass ceiling, focusing on what you don't have, focusing on the limitations, then you will be limited."

—Ava DuVernay

Day 313

"Champions keep playing until they get it right."

—Billie Jean King

Day 314

"I feel now that the time is come when even a woman or a child who can speak a word for freedom and humanity is bound to speak."

—*Harriet Beecher Stowe*

Day 315

"Whenever you are blue or lonely or stricken by some humiliating thing you did, the cure and the hope is in caring about other people."

—*Diane Sawyer*

Day 316

"We need to start work with the idea that we're going to learn every day. I learn, even at my position, every single day."

—Chanda Kochhar

Day 317

"I have chosen to no longer be apologetic for my femaleness and my femininity. And I want to be respected in all of my femaleness because I deserve to be."

—Chimamanda Ngozi Adichie

Day 318

"Whatever the problem, be part of the solution. Don't just sit around raising questions and pointing out obstacles."

—*Tina Fey*

Day 319

"Women are like teabags. We don't know our true strength until we are in hot water."

—Eleanor Roosevelt

Day 320

"We need to accept that we won't always make the right decisions, that we'll screw up royally sometimes—understanding that failure is not the opposite of success, it's part of success."

—Arianna Huffington

Day 321

"Don't let anyone tell you that you can't do something. Especially not yourself."

—Mindy Kaling

Day 322

"I don't think about beauty. I wake up and I want to be a smarter person, that's my focus. ... I'm encouraging certainly my girls that if they can make their inside and who they are really, really stunning then everything falls together."

—Angelina Jolie

Day 323

"The way I see it, if you want the rainbow, you gotta put up with the rain!"

—Dolly Parton

Day 324

"I try to live in a little bit of my own joy and not let people steal it or take it."

—Hoda Kotb

Day 325

"I always did something I was a little not ready to do. I think that's how you grow. When there's that moment of 'Wow, I'm not really sure I can do this,' and you push through those moments, that's when you have a breakthrough."

—Marissa Mayer

Day 326

"Of course I am not worried about intimidating men. The type of man who will be intimidated by me is exactly the type of man I have no interest in."

—*Chimamanda Ngozi Adichie*

Day 327

"And the day came when the risk to remain tight in a bud was more painful than the risk it took to blossom."

—Anaïs Nin

Day 328

"To me, fearless is not the absense of fear. It's not being completely unafraid. To me, fearless is having fears. Fearless is having doubts. Lots of them. To me, fearless is living in spite of those things that scare you to death."

—Taylor Swift

Day 329

"I have learned that as long as I hold fast to my beliefs and values – and follow my own moral compass – then the only expectations I need to live up to are my own."

—Michelle Obama

Day 330

"I do not wish women to have power over men; but over themselves."

—Mary Shelley

Day 331

"If you want something said, ask a man; if you want something done, ask a woman."

—Margaret Thatcher

Day 332

"If you think taking care of yourself is selfish, change your mind. If you don't, you're simply ducking your responsibilities."

—Ann Richards

Day 333

"You can never leave footprints that last if you are always walking on tiptoe."

—Leymah Gbowee

Day 334

"I do not wish women to have power over men; but over themselves."

—*Mary Shelley*

Day 335

"I'm learning how to drown out the constant noise that is such an inseparable part of my life. I don't have to prove anything to anyone. I only have to follow my heart and concentrate on what I want to say to the world. I run my world."

—*Beyoncé*

Day 336

"A strong woman is a woman determined to do something others are determined not be done."

—*Marge Piercy, poet*

Day 337

"You have to be consistent. You have to be yourself. You have to be committed to what you're doing. You have to not be afraid to be ambitious."

—*Roxane Gay*

Day 338

"Practice creates confidence. Confidence empowers you."

—Simone Biles

Day 339

"Take one day a week for yourself and go "off the grid." If smartphones are allowed to recharge, shouldn't we be allowed to as well?"

—Elizabeth Borsting

Day 340

"If you obey all the rules, you miss all the fun."

—Katharine Hepburn

Day 341

"Don't let the rejection deter you from staying confident in your venture."

—*Alexa Curtis*

Day 342

"If you don't stand for something, how can anyone respect what you do?"

—Miranda Lambert

Day 343

"It took me quite a long time to develop a voice, and now that I have it, I am not going to be silent."

—Madeleine Albright

Day 344

"'No' today doesn't mean 'no' tomorrow."

—Yvonne Orji

Day 345

"In order to create change of any kind, we have to first change the way we view ourselves."

—Alyssa Rosenheck

Day 346

"Once you've taken your seat at the table, it's your job to pull out a chair for the others, too. Look for the 'others.' Acknowledge them. Build a platform for them."

—Bianca Bass

Day 347

"Every day is a new opportunity to change your life and be who you want to be."

—Demi Lovato

Day 348

"Let your compassion fuel your passion."

—*Achea Redd*

Day 349

"Celebrate the wins in life but never be complacent."

—Danielle Takata

Day 350

"When people don't want the best for you, they are not the best for you."

—*Gayle King*

Day 351

"Character cannot be developed in ease and quiet. Only through experience of trial and suffering can the soul be strengthened, ambition inspired, and success achieved."

—Helen Keller

Day 352

"I have learned over the years that when one's mind is made up, this diminishes fear; knowing what must be done does away with fear."

—Rosa Parks

Day 353

"Money is a tool that helps us show up for the world in a bigger way."

—*Melody Pourmoradi*

Day 354

"You can show more of the reality of yourself instead of hiding behind a mask for fear of revealing too much."

—Betty Friedan

Day 355

"Don't compare yourself. Your inside self will compare to everyone's outside self when facing a growth opportunity or anything new. Don't listen to the doubt that follows. If you're compelled, go for it. You're already at no; don't be your own speed bump."

—Sue Hawkes

Day 356

"Nothing liberates our greatness like the desire to help, the desire to serve."

—Marianne Williamson

Day 357

"The question isn't who's going to let me; it's who is going to stop me."

—Ayn Rand

Day 358

"My best successes came on the heels of failure."

—Barbara Corcoran

Day 359

"Tolerance and compassion are active, not passive states, born of the capacity to listen, to observe and to respect others."

—Indira Gandhi

Day 360

"When I believe in something, I'm like a dog with a bone."

—Melissa McCarthy

Day 361

"Style is a way to say who you are without having to speak."

—Rachel Zoe

Day 362

"The most alluring thing a woman can have is confidence."

—Beyoncé

Day 363

"The success of every woman should be the inspiration to another. We should raise each other up. Make sure you're very courageous: be strong, be extremely kind, and above all be humble."

—Serena Williams

Day 364

"Be a girl with a mind, a woman with attitude, and a lady with class."

—*Anonymous*

Day 365

"When you undervalue what you do, the world will undervalue who you are."

—*Oprah Winfrey*

NOTES

www.ingramcontent.com/pod-product-compliance
Lightning Source LLC
LaVergne TN
LVHW081611080126
829370LV00013B/1035